I Love My Little Sister, I Think

Victoria Boyd

AuthorHouse™
1663 Liberty Drive
Bloomington, IN 47403
www.authorhouse.com
Phone: 1-800-839-8640

© 2010 Victoria Boyd. All rights reserved.

No part of this book may be reproduced, stored in a retrieval system,
or transmitted by any means without the written permission of the author.

First published by AuthorHouse 12/15/2010

ISBN: 978-1-4520-9640-7 (sc)

Library of Congress Control Number: 2010917708

Printed in the United States of America

Any people depicted in stock imagery provided by Thinkstock are models,
and such images are being used for illustrative purposes only.
Certain stock imagery © Thinkstock.

This book is printed on acid-free paper.

Because of the dynamic nature of the Internet, any Web addresses or links contained in this book may have changed since publication and may no longer be valid. The views expressed in this work are solely those of the author and do not necessarily reflect the views of the publisher, and the publisher hereby disclaims any responsibility for them.

I would like to give thanks to God for allowing me the opportunity to write and publish this book. I would also like to thank my loving family for being so supportive and my graphic designer Yasmean Graham. This book is dedicated to my late mother, Angela D. Bivens; you are truly missed.

Victoria

"Mom, I'm ready for Little Sister to come! When will she be here?" Danny said with great excitement.

"Soon enough, Son," said Danny's mom. "We have to be very patient, and she will come."

A day went by, and no Little Sister had arrived, so Danny asked again. "Mom, when will Little Sister get here?"

"Soon enough, son," Danny's mom said again.

Danny was so excited he could hardly contain himself. The next day he went to school and told all his friends that Little Sister was coming soon and that he was going to be a big brother.

After school Danny got on the school bus. He thought to himself, Maybe Mr. Wilson can tell me when "soon" is. After all, he was the one who told me all about frogs and how their job is to eat flies, so I didn't have to worry about killing them.

So Danny asked, "Mr. Wilson, when is soon?"

Mr. Wilson looked in his rearview mirror and said, "It could be today or it could be tomorrow." Oh, this made Danny very happy!

After getting off the school bus, Danny ran home as fast as he could. When he got to the kitchen, he saw his mom sitting at the table, so he ran up to her. He was out of breath and could hardly talk when he reached her. "Slow down and catch your breath," she said.

He stood there and panted like a dog. "Where's Little Sister?" he said, trying to catch his breath. "Is she in her room? Is she in your room?"

Danny's mom turned to Danny and said, "No, she's right here, still in my belly. See?"

Danny was angry. He said, "Mom, why don't you tell her to come out?"

She explained, "I could tell her to come out, but that wouldn't make her come any sooner."

Still angry, Danny stormed to his room and shut the door. He just didn't understand why his little sister would not come out. Besides, if she came out, he was going to share his toys with her.

When Danny's dad came home from work he saw that Danny's door was closed and that Danny wasn't playing in his playroom. So he opened Danny's bedroom door and saw Danny lying on the bed with his face in the pillow. He sat beside him, put his hand on Danny's shoulder, and said, "What's wrong, son?"

Danny turned to his dad with eyes full of tears and said, "It's not fair, Dad; it's just not fair."

"What's not fair, son?" Danny's dad asked.

"Little Sister will not come out to play with me, and I'm ready for her to come," Danny replied.

Danny's dad chuckled and said, "Son, you have to very patient; she will come when it's time for her to come."

"But, Dad, Mom says that she will come soon enough, and Mr. Wilson says that soon could be today or it could be tomorrow."

"Son, there's no need to be in a rush for Little Sister to come into the world. Babies have to grow while inside their mommy's tummy, and they don't come until they grow to the right size and are healthy. Don't you want her to be healthy?"

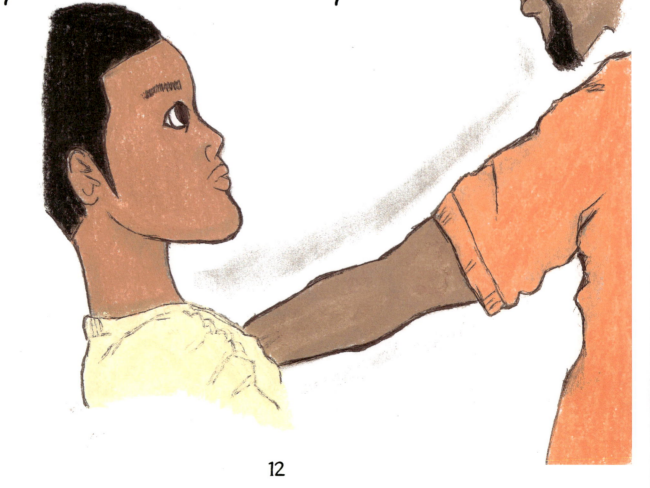

Danny thought to himself for a while and said, "I guess so, Dad." This made Danny feel a little better about waiting on his little sister to arrive.

A few weeks passed, and Danny calmed down. He was waiting patiently for his little sister's arrival. He'd already helped his mom and dad finish up her room and do the last-minute shopping that was left.

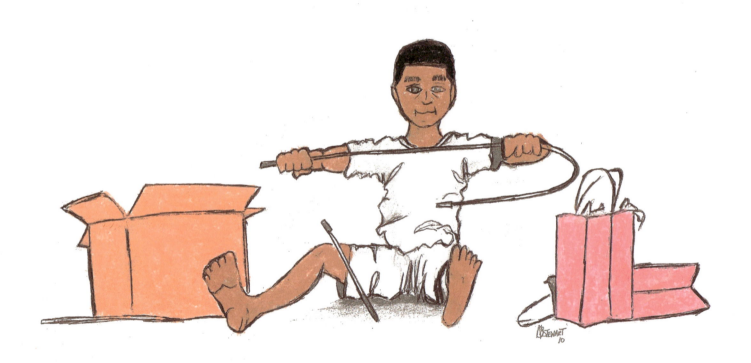

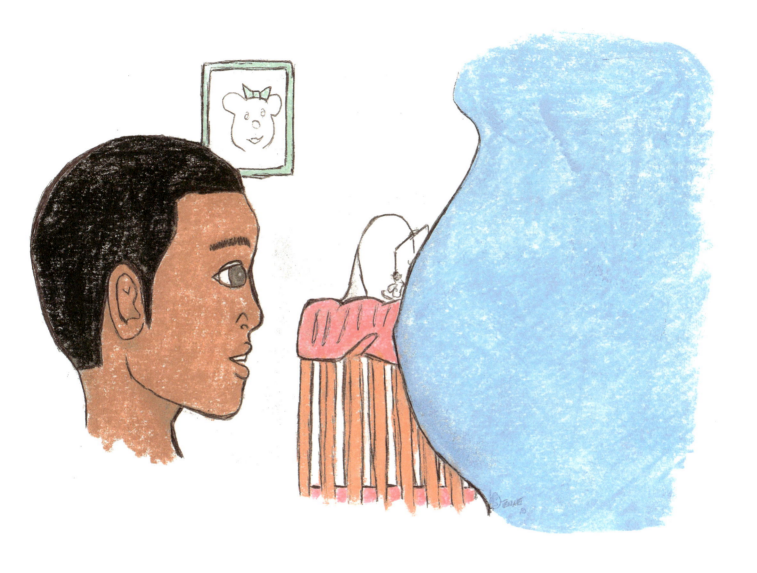

The day finally came when Little Sister was born and was ready to come home from the hospital. Danny waited at the door with Grandma and Papa for Mom and Dad to arrive with Little Sister.

Danny's dad walked through the door and said, "Danny, we're home!" Danny was so happy to see his mom, dad, and little sister.

"Let me see, let me see!" Danny walked beside his parents and into the living room.

He jumped up on the sofa beside his mom and just looked at his little sister. He thought she was so pretty, and she looked just like him.

A few hours passed, and the doorbell rang. Papa jumped up and quickly walked to the door. Uncle Matt and Aunt Julie walked into the living room after Papa and said, "Hi, Danny. How does it feel to be a big brother?"

Danny looked up at them and said, "It feels great. I love my little sister! Look at her; she looks just like me."

When the fifth guest left the house after seeing Little Sister, Danny began to feel a little left out. Everyone that stopped by spoke to him only once and then gave all of the attention that Danny was used to getting to his little sister. Why is no one talking to me anymore? Danny thought. Little Sister is getting all of the attention now, and I don't like it.

So Danny went into his mom and dad's room to ask. "Mom, Dad, why—"
But in the middle of Danny's sentence, his dad said, "Shh, not now, Danny. Mommy's trying to put Little Sister to sleep."
With tears in his eyes, Danny turned and walked back into his room. He sat down on the edge of his bed and said, "I love my little sister, I think."
Realizing that he'd cut Danny off in the middle of his sentence and sensing that Danny was a little jealous and confused, Danny's dad thought it would be a good idea for him to have a little talk with Danny. So he took him aside to reassure him that they still loved him very, very much and to explain that now they had to share their love with his little sister, because she was a part of the family too. This made Danny feel much better, so he promised his parents that he was going to be a helpful big brother and share his love with his baby sister too.

Lightning Source UK Ltd.
Milton Keynes UK
UKRC02n2214171116
287952UK00002B/3